Oxford Progressive English Readers provide a wide range of enjoyable reading at six language levels. Text lengths range from 8,000 words at the Starter level, to about 35,000 words at Level 5. The latest methods of text analysis, using specially designed software, ensure that readability is carefully controlled.

The aim of the series is to present stories to engage the interest of the reader; to intrigue, mystify, amuse, delight and stimulate the imagination.

GULLIVER'S TRAVELS

A VOYAGE TO LILLIPUT

Jonathan Swift

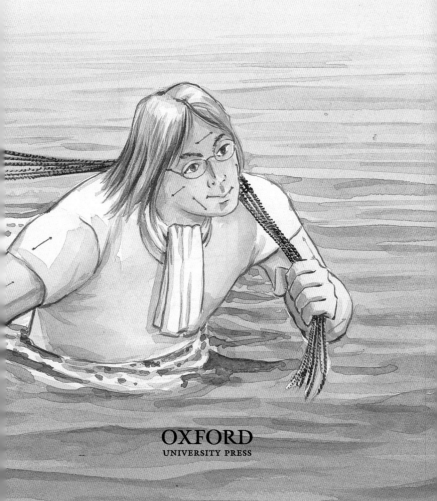

OXFORD
UNIVERSITY PRESS

OXFORD

UNIVERSITY PRESS

Oxford University Press is a department of the University of Oxford.
It furthers the University's objective of excellence in research, scholarship,
and education by publishing worldwide. Oxford is a registered trade mark of
Oxford University Press in the UK and in certain other countries

Published in Hong Kong by
Oxford University Press (China) Limited
39th Floor, One Kowloon, 1 Wang Yuen Street, Kowloon Bay,
Hong Kong

ISBN: 978-0-19-597136-1

21

Acknowledgements:
Illustrated by K H Cheung, Reader
Syllabus design and text analysis by David Foulds

Contents

Introduction

Gulliver's Travels — A Voyage to Lilliput is a story about adventures in a strange land. It is set in the eighteenth century.

In the story the main character is Gulliver, a ship's doctor. A great storm destroys the ship he is travelling on. Gulliver has to swim to save his life. He finds himself in a land where the people are no more than six inches tall and he is seen as a dangerous giant!

The story is told by Gulliver, and is written like a travel diary. He describes his adventures in the strange land of Lilliput.

A Voyage to Lilliput is the first book of *Gulliver's Travels,* a four-part story that was first published as *Travels into Several Remote Nations of the World.* You can read the second part, *Gulliver's Travels — Further Voyages* in Level 3 of this series.

Gulliver's Travels — A Voyage to Lilliput is a very popular adventure story for young people, but it also has hidden meanings. It is a satire, an entertaining political story. It was written to make fun of the leaders, life, and even religion, at the time.

Read on to find out more about Gulliver's adventures in Lilliput.

About Jonathan Swift

Jonathan Swift was born in Dublin, Ireland in 1667. His father died before he was born. Swift did not pay much attention to his school work, but he liked to read. He read a lot about things that he was interested in.

He is most famous for writing satires. Besides *Gulliver's Travels,* he also wrote shorter stories such as *A Tale of a Tub* and *A Modest Proposal.* In *A Modest Proposal* he writes a funny and, some say, horrible story. The story says that there are too many people in the world, and not enough food to feed them. Swift suggests a way to solve this problem. He suggests that the babies of poor people could be sold as food for rich people!

Because of this and other stories, people said that Swift hated mankind, and perhaps he was mad. What do you think?

1
A Ship's Doctor

A student of medicine

My father had five sons. I was the third. When I was fourteen he sent me to Cambridge to study. I was there for three years. Then he did not have enough money to pay my teachers any longer, so I went to London. 5

I wanted to be a doctor. In London I studied medicine with a famous doctor, Dr James Bates. While I was studying I worked for him, too, so my father did not have to pay him any money. There was one other 10 thing I wanted to do very much. I hoped to travel and visit foreign lands some day.

I loved reading. Of course, I liked to read about being a doctor. But I also read about science, mathematics, and engineering, which means knowing how to build 15 machines. Best of all, I liked reading about foreign countries, and the way people lived in other lands. When I had enough money, I bought books. But Dr Bates did not pay me much, so I could not buy many!

After four years I went home to see my family. I had 20 a pleasant surprise. My father and my uncle gave me forty pounds. Also they promised to send me thirty pounds each year while I learnt more about medicine. That does not seem to be much money these days, but in those days it was a lot. 25

So, at last, I had enough money to do what I wanted. I left Dr Bates and went to study at Leyden in Holland for two years. I still wanted to travel, so I learnt many things which I could use on long sea journeys, or 'voyages' as they are called. 30

My first voyages

After I finished studying at Leyden I became a ship's doctor. Dr Bates, my old teacher, advised me to take this job. He said it would be very good for me.

For three and a half years I sailed in a ship called the *Swallow*. I went on voyages from England to Turkey and other places. Then I decided to remain on land, in London, for a while. Dr Bates thought this was a good idea. He helped me, too. He sent many people who were ill to me, and I was often very busy.

I rented a house and later I married a young woman called Mary Burton. Her father gave us four hundred pounds as a wedding present. This, I thought, was a very useful present.

After two years my old friend and helper, Dr Bates, died. After that I did not have so much work to do. My wife and friends advised me to travel again.

I learn many new things

I sailed several times to Indonesia, which is a very long distance from England. These voyages lasted for six years and I earned a good amount of money. On these journeys I had plenty of time to read many interesting books. Some of them were new, while others had been written a long time before.

When we stopped in a foreign land I watched the people there very carefully. I noticed the special way they dressed and the special things they ate. I found out about their lives at home and at work. I found out about any special laws they had, and about the way their king or governors ruled them. In other words, I studied their 'customs'.

I also tried to learn their languages. My memory is good, so I learn new languages easily.

After six years, once again I became tired of the sea. I planned to stay at home with my wife and family. We moved to a different part of London, near the river Thames. 5

There is a great harbour there, which is always full of ships from every country in the world.

It was a busy place. All day and every day people worked in the harbour. Most of them put things on to ships, and took things from ships when they arrived. I 10 thought that many seamen and harbour workers would need a doctor. But my luck was not very good. I worked hard for over three years, but I only earned a little money. It was not enough for my family. So I took a good job on another ship, called the *Antelope*. This 15 ship was going to the South Sea Islands, in the Pacific Ocean.

A great storm

On 4th May 1699, we sailed from Bristol, a harbour on the south-west coast of England. We sailed west, and then south, into the great Atlantic Ocean. The weather was good all the way until we reached the south of Africa. We turned east, and then the weather changed. A great storm blew us to the north of Australia. This storm lasted a long, long time. Twelve seamen died. They had to work too hard, and because of the storm there was not enough food for them to eat. The rest of us were all very weak.

November was the beginning of summer in that part of the world, but the weather was bad all the time. It was cold, the skies were covered with clouds, and it rained a lot.

One morning the weather was worse than ever. The wind was blowing hard and driving us forward quite fast. It was raining, so we could not easily see where we were going.

Soon after ten o'clock, one of the men suddenly saw some rocks close to the ship. The seamen did their best to keep our ship away from the rocks, but the wind was too strong. It drove us towards them, and we hit them with a great crash. There was a lot of noise and shouting. People ran about the ship in all directions. No one knew what to do.

The ship was badly damaged. There was a large hole in one side, and sea water was coming through it. The ship started to go down. Five of the men and I put a small boat over the side of the ship, into the sea. Quickly, we got into the small boat and rowed away from those dangerous rocks. Soon after that, we looked back and saw the *Antelope* going down below the waves.

We rowed for about ten miles, but then we became tired. We could not row any more. Our little boat just went in any direction that the wind and waves drove it.

Suddenly, the wind started blowing much more strongly. It hit our boat and turned it over. We were all thrown into the sea. I never saw any of my companions again.

Close to death by drowning

I swam and swam. The wind and the waves helped to move me along. I allowed my legs to drop sometimes, but I could not feel any rocks or land below me. I wanted to stop and rest because I was so tired.

After an hour or two I could swim no more. I was ready to stop. If I did, then I knew that I would go down below the waves and die in the sea by drowning. I stopped swimming. I went under the water a little way. Then, to my surprise, my feet touched land!

I kept swimming forward. From time to time I tried to touch the land with my feet again. As I moved forward I found I could touch the land with my feet more and more easily.

5 Slowly the water became shallower and shallower. After I had swum about two miles I found that I was able to walk. Then, after I had walked for another mile, I saw land in front of me, and got to the shore.

When I reached dry land it was about eight o'clock 10 in the evening. I could not see any people or houses and I was too weak and tired to look for any.

The grass on the beach was the shortest and softest I had ever seen. That seemed strange, but I did not give it much thought. I just lay down on it. I was so hungry 15 and tired that I felt half-dead. I fell asleep at once.

2
A Prisoner

Tied to the ground

I slept very well for about nine hours. When I woke up, I tried to get on to my feet, but I could not move. My arms and legs were tied to the ground. My long, thick hair also seemed to be tied down. I could feel several thin pieces of string across my body from my neck down to the top of my legs. The only part of my body that I could move was my eyes.

The sun soon became hot and bright. As it moved slowly across the sky it began to shine on to my face. The bright light hurt my eyes. It was very painful to keep them open, and I could not move my head, so I had to close them.

I could hear a lot of noise around me. Many things were moving about. But I could not see what they were. When I opened my eyes I could only see the sky and the bright sun.

After a time I felt something on my left leg. It was alive and it moved very gently over my body towards my chin. I tried to look down as far as I could.

Suddenly I saw something. There, in front of me, standing on my body, was a very, very small man. He was only about six inches tall. He was holding a bow with an arrow in it, and he had more arrows in a bag on his back. Then I felt about forty more little people climbing over me.

This was the biggest surprise of my life. I could not believe it. I was so surprised that I shouted very loudly, and all the little people ran away. They were very frightened. Many jumped to the ground. Some of them were hurt quite badly when they fell off my body.

I try to get free

⁵ But soon these little men came back. One of them came very close, as he wanted to see my whole face. He lifted up his hands and eyes to show that I pleased him very much. Then he called out in a high and clear voice. I could not understand his language. The others ¹⁰ repeated his words. I did not know what they were saying.

While I was lying there I began to feel more and more uncomfortable. My arms and legs hurt because I could not move them. I tried hard to get free. I broke ¹⁵ some of the strings. Then I pulled some pieces of wood, called stakes, out of the ground. The strings had been tied to these stakes. My left arm was free! At the same time I pulled hard on the left side of my head. It was very painful but I loosened some more stakes that held ²⁰ down my hair. Now I was able to turn my head about two inches.

The little people shoot arrows at me

As I was doing this the little people ran away. I did not have time to catch even one of them. I heard someone shout an order in a loud voice. At once about one hundred arrows were shot through the air at me. I did not feel the arrows that went into my clothes, but I did feel those that went into my face and my left hand. These felt like sharp needles and were very painful.

I shouted with pain. I covered my face with my left hand and I tried to break all the strings. I wanted to get free but the little men shot more arrows. Some also tried to push their spears into me.

Luckily my jacket was made of a very strong cloth. Their spears were not sharp enough to go through that, so most of them did not hurt me.

I decided to lie still until night-time. My left hand was not tied so I thought it would be easy to get free later. As soon as it was dark I would be able to get away. When I was standing up I was sure that I could beat the little soldiers who were left to watch me.

But my plan was not needed. When the little people saw that I was lying still they stopped shooting.

A small man speaks to me

Soon after this I began to hear a knocking sound about four yards from my head. It made me think that someone was making something. My hair was still
5 loose on one side, so I could turn my head a little way. After a while I moved it very carefully, and very slowly. I did not want to frighten the soldiers again.

I saw that some of the little people had built a platform. They had used small pieces of wood, each
10 one about the size and shape of a ruler. The top of the platform was about eighteen inches from the ground.

Four people were standing on the platform. When I had turned my head a little more, so that I could see them easily, one of the four began to speak. He was
15 taller than the others and he seemed more important, too. I could not understand anything he said, but it looked as if he was speaking to me.

Sometimes his voice sounded kind. Sometimes he sounded angry. I tried to speak to him but, of course, we
20 could not understand each other.

All this time I was in pain because it was so hot. I lifted my hand to protect my face from the sun. Then I opened my mouth and pointed to it because I was hungry. The man who had been speaking understood
25 that. He knew what I wanted.

I am given food and drink

He left the platform and ordered some people to place ladders against my sides. They did this at once.

More than a hundred men climbed up the ladders.
30 They carried baskets of meat. The meat in each basket came from a different animal. I did not know the names of these animals at all. There were many different

shapes but each piece was smaller than the wings of a little bird.

I ate two or three pieces in one mouthful. Their loaves of bread were as small as beans. I ate them three at a time and they fed me as fast as they could. 5

I showed them that I was thirsty. They thought about this for a little time. They did not have any cups or glasses that were big enough for me. Then someone had a clever idea. They rolled a barrel close to my head and they knocked off its top. I could just reach it with my 10 free hand.

I lifted up my head a little, opened my mouth, and drank. I thought the barrel would have water in it, but I was wrong. It held about half a pint of wine which had a very pleasant taste. I emptied the whole barrel with 15 one big swallow.

The little men hurried to me with another barrel. I emptied that one very quickly, too, as I was so thirsty.

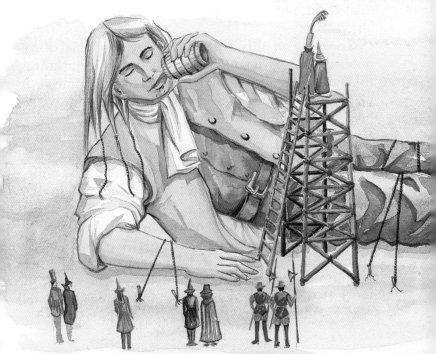

Then I moved my head to ask for another. But there was no more. I had drunk all their wine!

The little people were very pleased because I had eaten their food. They shouted and danced up and down on my body. Next they asked me to move the empty barrels for them. Everyone stood back, out of the way. With my left hand I threw the barrels to them. They all shouted with joy and surprise when they saw me throw these very heavy barrels so easily.

Secretly I wanted to throw down the forty or fifty soldiers who were standing on me, too. But I did not do this as they had been so kind to me. Also I remembered the pain from their pointed arrows and spears.

I remain a prisoner

I thought these little men were very brave. To them I must have looked very dangerous. I was ten times larger than them, but they walked all over me and were not afraid.

The king of this strange country sent one of his noblemen to see me. As soon as I had finished my meal, this nobleman came to talk to me. First he climbed up on my foot, then he moved along my body with twelve men behind him. In his hand he was carrying orders from the king. When he reached my face he spoke to everyone in a loud voice. He waved his papers and pointed his fingers. I found out later that he was telling me where to find the most important city in that country, their capital city.

He seemed to ask me a question. I answered quickly but nobody understood my words. I pointed to the strings round my body. I wanted him to tell the soldiers to untie them. I wanted to be free. But he shook his head. He placed his own hands and feet together to tell me that I was a prisoner. He pretended to eat and to drink. At first I did not know what he meant. Then I understood. I could have food but I could not have my freedom.

This made me angry. I tried to break the thin ropes and string. At once, hundreds of arrows were shot at me. Lots of them went into the skin of my hands, which began to feel very sore and painful. I lay still and decided not to frighten the little people again. It was true, they were much smaller than me, but I was their prisoner.

3
The Journey to the City

The Emperor's plan

Many people now came to look at me. The ropes on my left side were loosened a little and I turned on to my right side. They tried to be kind, for they rubbed
5 some oil on my hands and my face. The oil smelled very good, and the pain I was feeling from the arrows quickly went away.

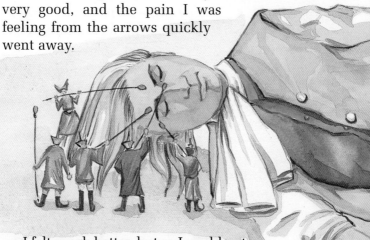

I felt much better, but as I could not
10 move much, and as the day was hot, I soon fell asleep again. I slept for about eight hours. I slept for such a long time because they had put something in the wine they had given me to drink.

A few weeks later, when I had learnt to speak their
15 language, I found out that the king, who was called 'the Emperor' by his people, had planned everything. That morning, some of the soldiers had told him about the very tall man they had found lying on the grass near the

beach. He thought that I might be very dangerous. He had ordered that I must be tied down. He had sent the food and wine. He had told them to put something in the wine to make me sleep. He also told the people to bring a machine which could carry me to the capital city. 5

The moving platform

These little people were very clever at mathematics. They were very good engineers, too. They could make machines that worked very well. They often used machines with wheels to carry long, heavy goods. 10

One thing that they used these machines for was to carry ships. They built their ships in the forests because there were plenty of trees for wood there. Then they carried these ships, which were often as much as nine feet long, on the wheeled machines from the forests 15 to the sea. Now they planned to bring the strongest and biggest wheeled machine in the kingdom to carry me to the city!

Four hundred woodworkers and engineers were ordered to get this machine ready, and to bring it to the 20 shore where I had been tied down. The machine looked like a platform, made of wood, about seven feet long and four feet wide. It was three inches from the ground and it had twenty-two wheels.

It was brought very close to my side. The little 25 people planned to move me on to the platform. But I did not know anything about it. I was asleep the whole time that they were doing this work.

I am taken to the capital city

Eighty sticks, each twelve inches long, were fixed in the 30 ground around me. The workmen fastened strong ropes round my neck, body, arms and legs. Nine hundred of the Emperor's strongest men pulled these ropes which went round little wheels, called pulleys, on the tops of the sticks. They pulled and pulled for about three hours. Slowly they lifted me up. When I was high enough above the ground, the wheeled platform was moved under me. Then, very carefully, very gently, I was put down until I was lying, still fast asleep, on the top of the platform.

One thousand five hundred horses, all about four and a half inches high, began to pull the platform towards the capital city. It was half a mile away.

When we had been travelling for about four hours I woke up. However, I was woken up in a very strange way. This is how it happened.

Something went wrong with the platform, and it stopped so that the engineers could mend it. While they were working, five young men decided that they would like to look at me when I was sleeping.

They climbed on to my body and then on to my face.
One of them, an officer in the army, put his spear into
my nose. That made me sneeze loudly, and I woke up.

The platform is mended

The young men ran away so quickly and so quietly   5
that I never saw them. I did not know why I had woken
up. About three weeks later someone told me all about
my journey on the wheeled machine, and about how
the young men had woken me. Nearly everyone had
thought it was very funny. But not the six young men: 10
they were frightened by the noise of my sneezing.

When the machine was mended we started moving
again. All through the rest of that day, the horses, the
platform with me tied on to it, and the army of little
people, moved slowly towards the capital city.   15

When night came, we stopped. Many of the people
went to sleep, but five hundred soldiers stood round
me, watching. Half of them were holding torches so that
they could see me easily. The other half were ready to
shoot their arrows if I moved.   20

The next morning, as soon as the sun was up, they
started pulling the platform again. I was still lying on it,
but by that time I was awake. At midday we arrived at
the city. We stopped about two hundred yards from the
city's main gate.   25

My new house

The Emperor, with all his followers, came out to meet
us. He wanted to talk to me, but a group of important
noblemen would not allow the Emperor to climb on to
me. They said that I was too dangerous.   30

On one side of the road, there was a tall, narrow building. It was five feet high. The Emperor and his followers climbed up there to look at me. About one hundred thousand people also came from the city to see me.

I think that during that day ten thousand people climbed over my body to look at me. The soldiers tried to stop them but there were too many people, and too few soldiers. Then an order came from the Emperor. His soldiers were told to kill anyone else who climbed over me.

There was an old temple close to us, opposite the tall, narrow building. Inside the temple there was just one very large room. It was the largest room in their kingdom.

Many years ago someone had been cruelly killed in the temple, so the people did not use it for praying to their gods any more. All the pictures of their gods and all the tables and chairs had been taken away.

The building was large, empty, and no one used it, so the Emperor had decided that I could live there. The main door of this building was four feet high and two feet wide. He thought I would be able to get in and out of the building quite easily.

My house is my prison

On each side of the door there was a small window, about six inches from the ground. The Emperor sent some workmen with ninety-one iron chains. They put the chains through one of the windows, brought them back through the door, and then locked both ends of each chain on to my leg. Thirty-six special locks were needed to fasten these chains on to me.

The workmen made sure that I could not break the chains. When this was done, they cut off all the strings and ropes that had been tying me down.

I sat up. All the people shouted with surprise. They knew I was very big, but when they saw me sitting up, I seemed bigger than ever. Then I stood up. They shouted even louder.

The chains were about six feet long. They were fastened to my left leg and to the temple, between the window and the door, so I could walk about in a half-circle. I was very happy to be able to get up and move. I had been tied to the ground, and to the platform, for almost two days. My arms and legs felt very stiff.

I went into the temple. I found that I could lie down easily in there. When I sat up, my head was about six inches below the ceiling.

I was pleased because these people were so kind
to me. To them I was very big and very dangerous. But
if I did not frighten them, I knew now that they would
give me food and drink. They had hurt my hands and
face with their arrows, but when I was quiet they had
given me oil to take the pain away. When they saw I
could not run away they allowed me to get up and
move about, and they had given me one of their largest
buildings to live in. But I was sad because I was still a
prisoner.

4
The Emperor of Lilliput

The Emperor comes closer

When I stood up I could see the beautiful country all around me. The fields, about twelve yards square, were like flower gardens to me. The tallest trees in the forest were only a foot taller than I was. The town looked like a painted picture.

The Emperor came down from the tall building where he had been watching me. He got on his horse and rode towards me, but the horse was very frightened. It jumped up on its back legs. The Emperor was a very good rider and did not fall. His followers ran to him and held the horse until it was quiet. Then the Emperor got down.

He walked round and round me but he stayed at a safe distance! He ordered food and drink. His cooks and servants brought these in boxes which they could push along. I emptied twenty boxes which were filled with food and ten filled with drink. Each box held only two or three mouthfuls.

The Emperor and his family

The Emperor's wife, the Empress, and their children, the young princes and princesses, sat on chairs a short distance away from me. When the Emperor got down from his horse, they came and stood by him.

The Emperor was taller than any of his noblemen. He was taller by about half an inch. His face showed that he was strong and brave. His body was straight and

he moved well, in a light and easy way. He was twenty-eight years old, which the people in that country thought was quite old. He had been emperor for seven years, and most people said that for all that time he had
5 ruled his country happily and well.

I lay flat on the ground so that I could see him more easily. Later, when he knew me better, he often stood on my hand and I could look at him very closely. Because of that, I am sure that I can describe him correctly.

10 His clothes were plain and simple. They looked half-Asian and half-European. On his head he wore a gold helmet. This helmet had beautiful birds' feathers and valuable stones of different colours on it. He held his sword in his hand so that he
15 could fight me if I broke my chains. This sword was three inches long and the gold top was covered with small, bright stones, called diamonds.

The Emperor's followers and all the ladies wore rich and beautiful clothes. There were so many of them that the ground where they were standing looked like gold and silver cloth.

We have language problems

That afternoon, His Majesty, the Emperor, and I spoke to each other. The Emperor spoke in a small, high voice. I could hear his words clearly, but I could not understand him. He could not understand a single word I said, either. I tried words from many languages — Dutch, French, Spanish, Italian and Latin. No one could understand my words, not even the cleverest of the Emperor's followers.

After about two hours the Emperor left. His wife, children and their servants went also, and so did the noblemen and their families.

There were strong soldiers all around me. A very large number of people had come to see me. The soldiers were there to stop the people from hurting and annoying me.

The people came as close to me as they could. Most of them just wanted to look, but a few tried to shoot arrows at me when I was sitting outside my house. One arrow just missed my eye.

A kind deed

An officer told the soldiers to catch six of the men who had been annoying me. The soldiers tied the hands of these men behind their backs. Then the six were brought to me. I had to choose how to punish them.

I put five of them in my pocket. Then I pretended that I was going to eat the sixth man.

The poor man screamed with very great fear. The soldiers, too, were afraid. I took out my knife. When they saw that, they thought that I was going to cut the poor man into pieces. But I only cut the rope round his
5   hands. Then I put him on his feet and I let him go free. I lifted the other five men out of my pocket, set them free, and put them gently on the ground too. The people and the soldiers were very pleased with my kindness.

That night I crept inside the temple. I lay down on the hard
15 ground to go to sleep. I did not sleep well. Two weeks later, the people made a bed for me. They joined six hundred of their little beds together to make one bed that was big enough for me.

The Emperor's advisers

20 The news about me spread through the country. Everyone wanted to come to the capital city to see me. All the villages in the land became empty.

This was a great problem. The farms needed the farm workers. If the farm work was not done, there would soon be no food to eat. So the Emperor ordered the village people to return to their homes. If people wished to stand near the temple looking at me, they had to pay some money to the Emperor's servants.

At the same time the Emperor asked some of his noblemen to advise him about me. They told him that they were afraid of what I might do. They thought that if I broke my chains I would be very dangerous. Also, I was eating so much food that soon all the people would be very hungry. The farmers could not grow enough food to feed all of the people of the capital city, and me, too.

These advisers thought that I should be killed. But then, they said, there would be another problem: what could they do with my body? They would not be able to make a hole in the ground that was large enough for it. So, my dead body would soon smell very bad and that might cause many people to become ill.

The Emperor decides I am not dangerous

While the advisers were talking, one of the noblemen told the Emperor about my kindness to the six men. When he heard about this, he was very pleased. He decided that I was not as dangerous as his advisers were saying, and he sent them away.

He ordered all the people from the villages near the capital to bring food to me. Every morning they brought six cows, forty sheep, bread, wine and other necessary things. The Emperor ordered his officers to make notes about all this food. Later the villagers were paid for it by an officer who looked after all the money in the kingdom.

I was given six hundred servants and they lived in small huts near me. Three hundred tailors made some clothes for me. They looked the same as the clothes that everyone else was wearing in that country. Six of the greatest teachers taught me their language.

Every morning, the Emperor, his noblemen and soldiers rode their horses close by me. The Emperor ordered this so that the horses would grow less frightened when they saw me.

I study the language

After about three weeks, I knew some of the language. I found out that the name of their country was 'Lilliput', and their capital city was called 'Milendo'.

The Emperor often visited me to see how I was getting on and sometimes he taught me himself. I learnt to say the words 'please set me free'. Every day, when he came, I got down on my knees and asked the same thing. He always replied something like this: 'I cannot do this yet. You must promise that you will not make war in my country. We will look after you well. We hope you will do your best to become our true friend.'

I began to think that I would be a prisoner of these little people for the rest of my life.

5

Inside Gulliver's Pockets

Two officers look through my pockets

One day, the Emperor wanted his officers to see if I was carrying any dangerous things. Many of the people came out from the city to watch.

'The law says that two officers must do this,' the Emperor told me. 'They cannot look at your clothes easily without your permission. Please help them and do not hurt them. If the officers take anything away they will return it to you when you leave our country. Or we will pay you for it.'

Two officers came to me. I lifted them up and I placed them in my coat pockets. Then I moved them into most of my other pockets. I had one secret pocket. I thought that if they did not find it for themselves I would not tell them about that one.

The two men wrote down on a sheet of paper the names of the things they found, and what they thought they were. When they had finished they gave the paper to the Emperor. This is what they wrote.

The things found in my pockets

'First we looked in the right pocket of the coat of the Great Man Mountain (I believe this is the meaning of Quinbus Flestrin, which was what they called me). We could only find one very large piece of cloth. It is large enough to cover the floor in a room in the palace. We think this must be the Man-Mountain's handkerchief.

'In the left pocket we found a large box, made of a bright, white-coloured metal. We think the metal is silver. We asked the Man-Mountain to open the box. There was a lot of dust inside. One of us stepped into it and this caused the dust to fly about. It made us both sneeze and sneeze.' (This dust was snuff, a kind of powder made from tobacco, and the box was my snuff box).

'In another pocket we found many sheets made of something stiff and white. Each sheet is as big as three men. They are tied together with a thick rope. On the sheets there are many strange, black marks which we think must be the Man-Mountain's way of writing. Each mark is half as big as the palm of our hands.' (A few envelopes with letters inside them.)

'We found a kind of machine that has about twenty long sticks on the back of a longer, thicker stick. It looked like the railings round Your Majesty's garden.

We do not know what this machine is made of. It might be bone. If it is, then the animal it comes from is larger than the Man-Mountain himself. We think this must be what the Man-Mountain uses to comb his hair.

'In the right pocket of his leg-clothes (they did not know the word for trousers) we saw a machine made from a long piece of iron. This is about the same height as one of us. There is a hole going all the way through it, from one end to the other. There are two more pieces of iron fixed on to this, and all the iron pieces are fastened together on to a piece of wood. We do not know what this machine is for, or how to use it. There is another in the left pocket.' (These were my guns.)

My knives, watch and money

'In the same pockets we found a few large pieces of metal. They are round, and flat, like plates. Some are silver and some are a red-brown colour. They are different sizes. On some of them we could see the picture of a man's head. They are very heavy and we could not lift them easily.' (My silver and copper coins.)

'There are also two black things. We could not reach the top of them. But we could see that they held flat pieces of a very hard, light-coloured metal. We think it is a special kind of iron, called "steel". The Man-Mountain told us that he uses one to cut his meat. He uses the other to cut the hair on his face.' (My knife and razor.)

'We found, hanging from one front pocket a long chain made of thick circles of silver. It has a very strange machine at the bottom. This machine looks like a flat ball. Half of it is made from silver and the other half is made from a strange metal that looks like water. We could see right through this metal.

'The machine makes a noise like a heart beating. We think that perhaps it contains a god in the Man-Mountain's religion. We think it holds a god because the Man-Mountain says before he does anything he always looks at this machine. It seems to tell him when to do things.' (My watch.)

'In the opposite pocket there is a big bag. It is filled with large pieces of yellow metal. The Man-Mountain must be very rich if these pieces are made from gold.' (My gold coins.)

My sword, gunpowder and bullets

'Round his waist the Man-Mountain wears a belt made from the skin of a very large animal. A sword is hanging on this belt. The sword is as big as five tall men.

'We found another bag hanging from the belt on the other side of the Man-Mountain. It is divided into two parts, each big enough to hold three or four men. We found heavy metal balls in one part. Each ball is as big as a man's head, and very difficult for one person to lift up. (Bullets for my gun.) In the other we found black powder.' (My gunpowder.)

'This is exactly what we found on the Man-Mountain's body. The Man-Mountain helped us to look in his pockets. He was very polite as he knew that we were Your Majesty's officers.'

The Emperor shows interest

When all this had been read aloud to His Majesty he asked me gently to give everything to the officers.

First he asked for my sword. He said he wanted to see it, and he asked me to take it out of its cover. At the same time he ordered three thousand of his soldiers to come closer. Their bows and arrows were ready to shoot at me.

The sea water had not damaged the sword very much and most of it was very bright. I waved it around and the soldiers shouted loudly. They were surprised and quite frightened, because my sword was shining like fire in the sunlight.

The Emperor, who was a very brave man, was not so frightened. He told me to put my sword away in its cover. This I did and then I placed it on the ground.

Next he asked for 'the iron with the hole in it'. He wanted my gun. I pulled it out of my pocket. He wanted to know what it was, and how to use it. I tried to explain, but no one in that country knew anything about guns, so the Emperor could not understand very well.

I said I would shoot my gun, if he wished. His Majesty agreed to this. I told him not to be frightened. Then I put gunpowder in the gun, but I did not put a bullet in it. I did not want to hurt anyone. I pointed the gun to the sky. There was a loud bang. Hundreds of people fell down as though they were dead. The Emperor did not fall over, but he looked quite frightened for a long time.

I placed my guns with my sword and I gave them my bag of gunpowder and bullets. I did not know all the correct words to use but I asked the officers to be careful with the gunpowder. I told them that if they put it in the Emperor's storehouse and let a flame touch it, there was enough powder to destroy the whole of the Emperor's palace.

The Emperor looks at my watch

The Emperor was very interested in my watch. He ordered two soldiers to carry it to him. They hung the watch on a thick piece of wood. Then each one carried one end of the piece of wood on their backs. He was surprised at the noise which never stopped. He liked the minute-hand. He could see it moving, for his eyesight was much better than mine.

He asked all his advisers and noblemen
what they thought my watch was.
They gave him many different
and strange answers.

I showed the Emperor my silver and copper money, and my purse with nine gold pieces in it. He looked carefully at my knife, my razor, comb, snuffbox, handkerchief and letters. The sword, guns and gunpowder were taken to His Majesty's storehouse. He gave all the other things back to me.

The two officers never found my secret pocket. In it I kept one or two small things that I knew would be of no interest to the Emperor, and my spectacles and my telescope. The spectacles I used to help me read. The telescope could make things that were far away look very close, and was very useful at sea. I did not want to lose either of them, and I did not want them to get broken.

A strange black animal

At about this time some people came to the king to say they had found something very strange on the sea shore. It was quite close to the place where I had first fallen asleep. This thing was large and black. It covered a space as big as the Emperor's bedroom, and it rose up in the middle as high as a man.

At first they had been very frightened of it, because they thought it was some kind of dangerous animal from the sea. But after they had watched it for a while they saw it did not move. They went close, and climbed on top of it. When they jumped up and down on it they heard a low noise. This made them think that under the top there was nothing but a large empty space.

In the end they thought this strange black thing might be something that belonged to the Man-Mountain. They asked the Emperor for five horses, so that they could pull it to my house.

As soon as I heard about it, I knew that they had found my hat. I thought when they were pulling it along the ground they would tear it. But the ground in Lilliput is smooth and flat, and it was still good enough to wear when I received it.

6
Free at Last

The Lilliputians like me

I tried to behave very gently with the Lilliputians at all times, and I was always very polite to everyone. This pleased the Emperor, the noblemen, the army and nearly everyone who lived in that country. So I hoped that I should get my freedom soon.

Slowly the people lost their fear of me. I tried to be kind and friendly all the time. Sometimes I would lie down and let five or six of them dance on my hand. The boys and girls played games by running around on top of my head, and hiding themselves in my hair.

After some weeks I became quite good at their language. I could understand almost everything that was said to me. They could understand most of what I wanted to say to them. I often spoke to the Emperor and some of his chief servants.

Lilliputian games

The Emperor was so pleased with me that he agreed to let me watch some of their special games. I do not know of any country in the world that has games like these.

The first was a rope game. A long rope was tied up between two poles. It was about two feet long, and one foot above the ground. The people who played this game had to walk backwards and forwards along the rope, and even jump about and dance on it. The distance between the rope and the ground was twice the height of a Lilliputian, so this was quite dangerous.

The game is not just played to make people happy. It has a special use. When the Emperor is looking for someone to help him rule the country, many people come to play the rope game in front of him. Each person tries to be better than the others. Those who are the best at the rope game are given jobs in the Emperor's palace. Of course, all the Lilliputian parents would like their children to work for the Emperor, so everywhere in Lilliput you can see children practising the rope game.

The jumping game

Another game is only played in front of the Emperor, the Empress, and the Emperor's chief servant. It is played twice every year. A number of his most important noblemen are asked to play the game.

The Emperor places three long pieces of cloth on a table, one blue, another red, and the third green. These are prizes. Then he and the chief servant take a long stick. The Emperor holds one end and the chief servant holds the other end. Sometimes they hold it high above the ground, and sometimes they hold it low, and very close to the ground. The noblemen must jump over the stick when it is high. When it is low they must get down on their hands and knees and go under it. The three that can do this the longest, without falling over, are given the prizes.

The Lilliputians are very proud of these prizes. At special times when they wear their finest clothes, they also tie the coloured pieces of cloth around themselves. Then everyone can see that they are very good at this game.

I make some promises

I asked many times for my freedom. His Majesty spoke to his advisers about this. Nearly everyone agreed to set me free, but not the Emperor's Admiral, the chief officer on the Emperor's warships. He hated me. I did not know why. ₅

At last he, too, agreed with all the rest. He came himself to see me with several important officers.

This is what he told me to do. I had to hold my right foot in my left hand. Next I had to put the middle finger ₁₀ of my right hand on the top of my head and my thumb on the top of my right ear. Then I had to promise many things very seriously.

These were the promises.

First: *The Man-Mountain must not leave the* ₁₅ *Kingdom without permission. He may only leave if the Emperor allows him to.*

Second: *He must not enter the capital city without an order from the Emperor. He must tell the people about this two hours before he wants to go. Then they can remain at home where they will be safe.*

5 Third: *The Man-Mountain must use the chief roads. He must not lie down on the grass or in the farm fields.*

Fourth: *He must be very careful when he goes for a walk. He must not step on anybody, or on any horses* 10 *or small wheeled machines. He must not pick up any of the people of Lilliput without their permission.*

Fifth: *If the Emperor wishes to send a message to someone quickly, the Man-Mountain must help him.* 15 *He must carry the messenger and his horse in his pocket for a journey of six days. Then he must bring them back safely. And he must do this once each month.*

Sixth: *He must help the Lilliputians against their* 20 *enemies on the island of Blefuscu. He must help to destroy all their ships. These ships are getting ready to attack Lilliput now.*

Seventh: *The Man-Mountain must help the work- men to lift some heavy stones. These are needed for* 25 *walls in the city park.*

Eighth: *He must walk all round the island of Lilliput in two months' time. He must count his steps to find out the exact distance round the country.*

If he promises to do all these things, the Man- 30 *Mountain will be given food, as much as is needed for 1,728 people. He can visit the Emperor when he wants to. The Emperor promises to help him in many ways.*

I am free at last

I agreed to everything, though I did not like some of the promises. The Admiral still hated me and he gave me a lot of trouble.

The Emperor himself watched when my chains were taken off. 'I hope you will be a useful servant of our kingdom of Lilliput,' he said to me. 'I hope you will deserve my kindness now and in the future.' I bowed politely to him and thanked him. I was free at last.

Each day I now received as much food as 1,728 people of Lilliput could eat. I asked someone how they had worked out this number. He told me that the Emperor's doctors had measured my height. I was twelve times taller than anyone else there. So they decided that my body could hold at least 1,728 times as much food as theirs. Therefore the doctors had agreed that I needed 1,728 times more food!

I visit the capital city

I wanted to see Milendo, the capital city of Lilliput, very much. I asked for permission to visit it after I was set free.

The Emperor agreed at once. I promised not to hurt the people or their houses. Everyone was told about my visit and they were advised to remain indoors until I had left.

There was a big wall all round Milendo, two and a half feet high and one foot across. Every ten feet along this wall a tall building had been built. I stepped over the great west gate and I walked very slowly and carefully through the chief streets. I did not wear my coat as it was so long. It might damage the tops of the houses while I walked along. Thousands of people watched me from windows and the house tops. Some of the houses had as many as five floors each. They were almost as tall as me.

Milendo appeared to be the busiest city that I had ever seen. It is built in an exact square and each city wall is five hundred feet long. The chief streets divide it into four quarters. These streets are five feet wide. There are many lanes as well, but these are only twelve to eighteen inches wide. There seemed to be many good shops and markets for the five hundred thousand people who live there.

The Emperor's palace

The Emperor's palace is in the centre of the city, at the place where the two great streets meet. His Majesty gave me permission to step over the palace wall. The first building inside the palace wall is made to look like an open square, forty feet long on each side. Inside this building I could see two more square buildings, one inside the other. Between the square buildings were beautiful gardens. I was told that the building in the centre, the smallest of the three, contained the rooms of the Emperor and all his family.

I wanted to see these rooms very much, but it was very difficult to do this. The main gates from one building to another were only eighteen inches high and seven inches wide. The walls of the largest building were five feet high. I could not step over them, however, for I would have damaged them very much. The Emperor was disappointed at this, for he wanted me to see his beautiful home.

I have a plan

After some time, I thought of a plan. I cut down some of the largest trees in the park outside the city. Then I made two stools about three feet high. They were strong and I could stand on them.

I went to Milendo again. All the people remained inside their houses, as before, and I went to the palace with my two stools. When I reached the first building I stood on one stool. Next I lifted the second stool over the top of the building and put it down between the first building and the middle building. The gardens are about eight feet wide there.

Then I stepped from one stool to the other. I used a stick to pull up the first stool and I put the stool down again between the middle building and the third building. I stepped over again and there, in front of me, was the Emperor's palace.

The windows were wide open. I had to lie sideways to look inside. The rooms were very beautiful and I could see the Empress and her children. The Empress smiled and she put her hand out of the window. I kissed it because I wished to greet her politely and correctly.

Soon after that I returned to the temple, which was now my home and not my prison house.

7
The War

The two Lilliputian groups

About two weeks later, a very important officer of the king visited me. His name was Reldresal. He wanted to talk to me seriously about the kingdom of Lilliput.

Reldresal told me there were things happening in the country that he thought I did not know about. Lilliput was not such a happy country as it seemed. Two big problems were giving the Emperor a lot of trouble.

The first problem was that the Lilliputian people were divided into two big groups. These were called the Tramecksan and the Slamecksan. The word mecksan means heel, the back part of a shoe. The Tramecksan people wore shoes with high heels, and the Slamecksan people wore shoes with low heels.

All the Lilliputians belong to either the Tramecksan or the Slamecksan group. The groups hate each other. People in one group try not to eat, drink or even talk with people in the other group. Slamecksan children cannot play with Tramecksan children, and they have to go to different schools. If a Tramecksan boy falls in love with a Slamecksan girl, there is always a lot of trouble.

The Emperor and his noblemen at the palace were all in the Slamecksan group. 'Look at the Emperor's shoes next time you see him,' Reldresal said. 'The Emperor has the lowest heels in the country.'

The war between Lilliput and Blefuscu

The second problem was the war between Lilliput and the nearby country of Blefuscu. The war had been going on for almost three years. The Emperor was afraid
5 because there were many large and strong warships in the navy of Blefuscu, and thousands of brave men to sail them. Even now, Blefuscu was getting ready to attack the shores of Lilliput.

Reldresal told me that the trouble began long ago
10 when the Emperor's grandfather was a boy. The child wanted to eat an egg. The egg was in an eggcup, with the larger end up. The boy tried to break off the top of the egg with a knife, but he cut his finger. His father then said that everyone in Lilliput must put their eggs
15 in their eggcups the other way round, and break off the smaller end.

For hundreds of years, when Lilliputians had eaten eggs, they had always broken off the larger end. Many people did not want to change. They said that breaking
20 off the larger end was the only right way to eat an egg. All Lilliputians ate eggs that way. They said that if they did not break off the larger end of their eggs they would not be true Lilliputians any longer. They said the Emperor was wrong to make people do new things
25 without asking them about it first.

A lot of them fought against the Emperor in those days. Many Big-endians were killed. Many more ran away from Lilliput to Blefuscu, where they asked the King of Blefuscu to help them. Now the two countries
30 are fighting a war because of this.

'His Majesty ordered me to tell you all these things,' the officer said. 'He hopes that you will be grateful because he gave you your freedom. He hopes you will be ready to help Lilliput in any way.'

'Please tell His Majesty,' I replied, 'that I will do anything I can. I will even put my own life in danger, in order to fight the enemies of the Emperor and his kingdom.'

I find out about Blefuscu

Reldresal told me that Blefuscu was an island. It was north-east of Lilliput. The water between the two countries was only eight hundred yards wide.

No one in Blefuscu knew anything about me for they had not seen me. They were not allowed to speak to anyone in Lilliput.

Later, I told His Majesty that I was thinking of a plan to take all the ships of the enemy at once. These ships were in their harbour waiting for a good wind. I asked the cleverest Lilliputian seamen how deep the sea was between Lilliput and Blefuscu.

They talked about my question for a while. Then they told me that the deepest parts, in the middle, were about six feet deep. Nearer the shore, on both sides, it was never more than four feet deep.

I walked almost to the sea shore and hid behind a hill there. I took out the telescope from my secret pocket. I looked across the sea towards Blefuscu. There, in a large harbour, I could see all the ships of the Blefuscan navy. There were about fifty warships and a number of other ships to carry soldiers across the water.

I reach the enemy's ships

I returned to my house. I ordered bars of iron and thick, strong wire to be brought to me. The wire that they gave me was very thin. I made ropes, using three lengths of wire for each rope. I made hooks, twisting three iron bars together to make one hook. Altogether I made fifty hooks and fifty ropes. I fastened one hook to every rope.

Then I went back to the seashore. I walked out into the sea as far as I could. When the water was too deep for me to walk, I began to swim. I swam the rest of the way to Blefuscu, keeping my head very low in the water. Less than half an hour later I reached the enemy ships.

I stood up. The enemy were so frightened that they jumped out of their ships and swam to the shore. I fastened a hook to each ship and I tied all the ropes together at the other end.

While I was doing this, the soldiers of Blefuscu shot thousands of arrows at me. Many arrows stuck in my hands and face. These were very painful and I could not work quite as quickly after that. Luckily I was wearing my glasses. They protected my eyes against the arrows.

As soon as I had fastened all the hooks into the ships, I held on to the other end of the ropes. I pulled and pulled.

The enemy lose their ships

Nothing happened! The ships were fastened to iron hooks, called anchors, at the bottom of the sea. These anchors were at the other end of the ships. I could not move any of the ships, even though I pulled very hard. So I decided to break the ropes which held their anchors. This was very dangerous and difficult.

I walked back through the harbour water, round to the other end of the ships. About two hundred arrows went into my hands and face. The rest of my body was covered by the sea water. One by one, I broke each of the anchor ropes. Then I went back to the front of the ships.

I held the ends of the fifty
ropes together, and pulled
once more. This time all the enemy
ships came sailing along. I half-swam
and half-walked back to Lilliput.

    The people of Blefuscu could say nothing at first.
They were so surprised. They thought I was going to
destroy their ships or push them out to sea. Suddenly
they understood what I was doing. They saw that the
Blefuscu ships were all going to Lilliput. They began to
scream and shout very angrily. I cannot describe the
frightening, angry sounds I heard.

I become a Lilliputian nobleman

I stopped to pull out the arrows from my face and I came safely back to Lilliput. The Emperor and all his noblemen were waiting on the shore. At first they had
5 seen the enemy ships moving forward in a half-moon shape. But they could not see me, because I was swimming. Where was the Man-Mountain? Were these the enemy ships coming nearer and nearer? The Emperor was truly frightened. Soon after that, everyone
10 could see me. When the water was shallow enough, I held up the end of the ropes to which the ships were fastened.

'Long live the Emperor of Lilliput,' I shouted.

When I was standing on dry land, the Emperor
15 thanked me over and over again. He gave me a special title, Nardac, which meant 'Great Nobleman'. It was the highest title in the kingdom.

I anger the Emperor

Next he asked me to bring across the sea any Blefuscan
20 ships that I could find. He wanted to make Blefuscu a part of Lilliput. I did not wish to hurt the people of Blefuscu any more so I refused very politely. His Majesty never forgave me for this. He forgot that I had kept his country safe from danger for him. He forgot
25 that I had brought all the Blefuscu navy to him. He was angry because he wished me to destroy the enemy completely. His anger was so great that it almost caused my death a little later on.

However, I was able to help
30 him again. I thought that the Emperor would be very pleased with me after this.

A serious fire

One night I heard the cries of many people at my door.
They were shouting the word 'Fire' over and over again.
Several of the Emperor's servants asked me to hurry to
the palace. The room belonging to the 5
Empress was on fire.

I got up at once. The moon
was shining so I could
see clearly. I was very
careful and did not 10
touch anyone
on my way to
the palace.

All the people were passing buckets of water from hand to hand. I threw the water on the fire for them. But this was very slow, for they had to carry the water a long way. Each bucket was as small as an eggcup. The
5 flames were growing higher. We could not put them out. It seemed hopeless. The beautiful palace would be destroyed in front of me. Then I had an idea.

How the fire was put out

I ran towards the water. I got down on my knees and
10 filled my mouth with it. Then I spat this water over the fire. It was not very nice but it was the only thing I could do at the time. It was successful and in three minutes the fire was completely out. The lovely building was safe.
15 By then the night was over, and it was daytime. I did not wait to see the Emperor for a very good reason. Spitting was not allowed near the palace. Any person who did this would die. This was the law for everyone.

His Majesty sent me a message. He said that he was
20 ordering the chief law officer to sign a pardon for me. But this pardon did not come. The Empress hated the way in which I had put the fire out and kept her room safe from danger. She would not live in it again. I knew, therefore, that she would cause trouble for me.

8
Laws and Customs

The laws of Lilliput

In the kingdom of Lilliput there are many interesting laws and customs. The way they punish people is very cruel. They would tear to pieces anyone who hurts one of the Emperor's officers. Everyone there loves peace and order. 5

But the law also protects the helpless. It punishes anyone who wants to cause trouble. It says that most men can protect their goods from robbers. But many cannot protect themselves against wicked people who will cheat them. This is because cheats are often cleverer than most people. The punishment for cheating in Lilliput is the same as the punishment for robbery — death! 10

Once I tried to help a man. He had taken a lot of money from his master, but I asked the Emperor to forgive him. The Emperor was very surprised. He said that the man had done something wrong and therefore he must be punished. 15

I explained that the customs in my country were different. Sometimes a robber was not punished the first time he did something wrong. He was allowed to try to live a better life. But the Emperor thought this was not a good thing to do. 20

In Lilliput, if people obey all the laws for seventy-three months they are given some money. They can also add the name 'Law-keeper' to their family name. 25

I told the Lilliputians that in my country we punish people for breaking the law, but we do not give them anything for obeying the law. So they thought the customs and laws of my country were not as good as theirs.

The Statue of Justice

5   They took me to Milendo and showed me a statue. This was a large piece of stone which had been cut to look like a woman. They said that this was their Statue of Good Laws. In our country we would say, 'Statue of Justice'.

10   The face of Justice was very strange. It had six eyes — two in front, two behind and one on each side. This means that Justice is able to look all round her. She holds a bag of gold in her right hand. The gold

15 is to give to good people. But she carries a sword in her left hand. This is to punish wicked people.

In this country it is very

20 important to be good. When a man is looking for work, the way he behaves is more important than the things he can do. The people of Lilliput believe that a

25 well-behaved man will be able to do any kind of work. If, when he is working, he does something wrong, it will not be because he is planning some

30 wicked deed. He will not hurt anybody. But a clever, badly-behaved man will be a danger to everyone.

The Emperors of Lilliput have always said that they rule their country for God. Anyone who does not believe in their God is not allowed to work for the Emperor.

Men must show thankfulness to those who have helped them. The punishment for not being thankful is death. They think that people who do not love someone who has helped them cannot love anyone, not even the Emperor or their country.

The children of Lilliput

The people of Lilliput have a strange idea about children. They say that children do not ask to be born, so children do not belong to their parents. They belong to Lilliput. When children are twenty months old they leave their parents. They go to homes which are only used for babies and children. There they are looked after by special nurses and teachers.

The Lilliputians say that parents do not really want their children. Parents cannot care for them properly. There is so much trouble in the world that parents do not have time to think about their children. These special schools can look after children in the correct way.

In these special schools, children are taught how to behave well and how to think good thoughts. They do not study to pass examinations. Instead, they learn all about how to be good people and they learn to love their country. There are separate schools for the children of noblemen and for the children of working people. The girls and boys are in different schools or homes.

The children of noblemen wear simple clothes and eat plain food. Servants dress them until they are four years old, but after that they dress themselves. Even the

Emperor's children must dress themselves. The children are not allowed to talk to the servants. They must play with each other, and a teacher remains with them all the time.

How the children are taught

The parents of the children are allowed to see them twice a year. They may kiss their child when they first see him or her, and again when they are leaving. But a teacher stands nearby to see that the parents do not bring any toys or food. The parents may not even whisper any kind or loving words to them.

The Emperor's advisers decide how much money each family must pay to the school. Children of noblemen remain at school until they are fifteen. The schools for other boys and girls are almost the same. But they leave school when they are eleven years old. Then they begin to learn about their future work.

The schools for the daughters of noblemen are almost the same as the schools for their sons. Women servants dress the girls until they are five years old. The girls are taught to be brave and clever. They must be equal to the men when they are grown up. They learn to be useful, helpful and clever companions to their future husbands.

The girls return to their homes when they are old enough to marry. This is when they are about twenty-one. Their parents are usually very grateful to the teachers for all their care and kindness. The daughters from poor families are taught to do useful work. They learn to become wives, too.

There are no beggars in Lilliput. Old people and people who are ill go to the hospitals, which are all free.

Clothes are made for me

I stayed in Lilliput for nine months and thirteen days. I like to use my hands so I made a table and a chair. I used trees from the Emperor's park for them. Two hundred women-tailors made me some shirts to wear, some sheets for my bed, and some tablecloths. They used the strongest cloth they could find, but it was very thin. They sewed three pieces together, one on top of the other, to make it stronger.

The tailors measured me when I was lying on the ground. One stood on my neck, another stood on my waist. They held a piece of string between them. A third woman measured the length of the string. Her ruler was one inch long. They also measured my old shirt. When they had finished the measuring and the sewing, the new shirt fitted me exactly.

Three hundred men-tailors made some other clothes for me. This time I got down on my knees to be measured. A tailor let down a piece of string from my neck to the ground. This was the length of my coat. I measured my sleeves and waist myself. The clothes were made in my house because the other houses were too small. When my clothes were finished they looked very strange as the cloth was cut in so many different shapes and sizes.

My food costs too much

Every day three hundred men cooked my food. They lived with their families in little huts near my house. Each man cooked two dishes a day. I used to lift up twenty servants in my hand and put them on my table. A hundred more worked on the ground. Some carried the dishes of food while others carried the barrels of wine. The servants who were standing on the table pulled up all these things. One dish of their meat was equal to one mouthful for me. A barrel gave me a single drink.

One day His Majesty came to watch me while I ate. He was surprised to see that I could put twenty or thirty chickens on the end of my knife. I could eat big birds in a single mouthful.

But something bad happened. It was the result of the Emperor's visit to me. When he told his noblemen how much I ate, my enemy, the Admiral, said the cost of my food was too high. Lilliput did not have enough money to pay for it. There was not enough money to keep me alive.

Just after this, I did something very foolish. I told the Lilliputians that I wanted to visit the country of Blefuscu.

9
The Man-Mountain is in Danger

A secret visitor

At that time I did not know very much about kings and their followers. I had only heard stories about wicked noblemen in other countries. I did not think there were any in Lilliput. But it seemed that some people were making a secret plan against me. This is how I discovered it.

One evening, when I was getting ready for my trip to Blefuscu, someone knocked gently on the door of my house. My servant went to see who was there. He came back and told me that one of the Emperor's officers had come. He would not tell my servant his name. He just said that he must talk to me.

When I heard this I understood what he meant. This person had come to visit me secretly. He did not want anyone to know about it. I went to the door and saw an officer whom I had helped once.

The Emperor thinks I will destroy Lilliput

At once I lifted him up and put him in my pocket. Then I fastened the door. I told my servant that if anyone else came he should say that I was ill and that I had gone to sleep. I did not want to see anyone else that night.

I put my visitor, the officer, on the table. We greeted each other. He seemed to be very frightened about something. He asked me to listen to him carefully.

'Several secret meetings have been held,' he said. 'The Admiral has always hated you. The Emperor is angry with you because you would not destroy all the ships of Blefuscu. Now the Emperor is afraid that you are planning something in Blefuscu. He thinks you may be planning to destroy Lilliput.

'Many of the Emperor's men agree with the Admiral,' the officer continued. 'They have written down many things against you. They say you are unthankful. They say you are false to our Emperor and our country and many other things. They say that your punishment should be death. I have brought you a copy of the things they have written.'

What I had done wrong

He took out a long piece of paper and all this was written on it:

1. *By an old law, no one is allowed to spit in the palace gardens. The Man-Mountain spat there. He pretended to be putting out a fire.*

2. *The Man-Mountain brought back the ships from Blefuscu to Lilliput. The King, our Emperor, asked him to do this. Also, His Majesty asked him to destroy all the enemies of Lilliput. The Man-Mountain refused to do this. He pretended that the people of Blefuscu had done nothing wrong.*

3. *When messengers came to Lilliput from Blefuscu, he greeted them kindly. He helped these servants of the Emperor's enemies.*

4. *The Man-Mountain is planning to visit Blefuscu. He will help the Emperor of Blefuscu, who is the enemy of our Emperor.*

There were many other things on the paper, but these were the most important ones.

A plan to kill me

'His Majesty,' my visitor told me, 'does not wish to kill you. He wants you to leave Lilliput. But he does not want you to help his enemies in Blefuscu either.'

He told me that the Admiral had advised the Emperor to kill me at once. The Admiral wanted to put something bad in my food or shoot arrows at me.

But some of the others did not like this idea.

They said that the Emperor had given the Man-Mountain his freedom. They also said that the Man-Mountain had kept all his promises. Because of that, it would be cruel to kill the Man-Mountain.

One adviser hated the Man-Mountain because his food cost such a lot of money.

He had a clever, but cruel, plan. He said that the people of Lilliput would be proud of their king if the Emperor was kind to the Man-Mountain. He said that the Emperor should not kill him. He should just damage
5 the Man-Mountain's eyes so that he would not be able to see.

Then the Emperor could forgive the Man-Mountain. Without his eyesight, the Man-Mountain would not be dangerous. Also he would still be very strong. Soldiers
10 could tell him where to go and what to do, and he would be very useful to Lilliput. So, this adviser said, the people of Lilliput would think their Emperor was both clever and kind.

But the rest of the Emperor's advisers were very
15 angry, my visitor told me. The Admiral jumped to his feet and said, 'Do you want to help the Emperor's enemy? Do you want to allow him to live? This man put out a great fire by spitting. So, if he wants to, he can fill the palace with water and drown us all. He
20 pulled the ships of Blefuscu to our harbour. He can also take them away at any time. He is dangerous. He must die.'

How they will do it

My friend told these things to me very sadly.

25   'His Majesty does not want to kill you, but he wants to punish you,' he went on. 'Another officer said that we ought to give you less food. Then you would become smaller and smaller. At last you would be weak and you would die. Then we could cut your body into
30 small pieces. People could put these pieces in the ground in places that were far away from the city. There would not be any smell. They could keep your bones to show to people now and in the future.

'I am afraid that almost everyone agreed to this plan. Only the Admiral did not agree. He wants you to be killed at once!'

My friend went on to tell me what the plan was.

'In three days' time,' he said, 'an officer will come to your home. He will tell you that the Emperor and all his advisers are full of kindness. Twenty of the best doctors will come to take away your eyesight. You must be helpful and lie down on the ground. Then they can shoot their arrows into your eyes.

'This is what the officer will tell you. He will not tell you that they will stop giving you food, so that you will die later. He will just tell you that the Emperor is a good and kind friend to you.'

My brave visitor said that he must now leave my house secretly.

'Please think very carefully about my words,' he said as he was leaving. 'I hope you can plan something to help yourself this time.'

I thanked this true friend and put him gently outside my house.

I decide what to do

When my visitor had left I felt sad. At first I did not know what I ought to do.

The Emperor had a strange custom. At special meetings of his advisers he used to tell them that he was very kind. At once everyone knew that His Majesty was planning a cruel deed. I could not understand this. I did not think it was kind to take away my eyesight. It was cruel, not kind or gentle at all.

At first I thought of asking the Emperor to forgive me. The facts were correct. I had done these things. Perhaps he would be kind, but I knew that my enemies would not be kind. They would not allow him to be kind either.

Then I thought that I would fight the whole of the Emperor's army. I would throw stones at the city. I could destroy the whole city easily. Then I remembered something. All the people in Lilliput had been so kind to me. The Emperor had been kind to me, too.

At last I decided what to do. I would go to Blefuscu. I wrote to the Emperor's chief officer and told him this.

10
Gulliver Returns to England

I go to Blefuscu

Very early next morning I went to the harbour. I took one of the Emperor's ships and put all my clothes and goods in it. I jumped into the sea and swam to Blefuscu. Two villagers showed me the way to the capital city. I carried them with me until we were about two hundred yards from the city. 5

I asked the two villagers to tell the King of Blefuscu's officers about my arrival. I hoped they would arrange for me to see him. 10

After about one hour I got a reply. The King, with his family and his chief officers, was coming to see me.

Soon after that the King and his family arrived. They were not frightened of me at all. I lay on the ground to kiss the hand of the King and the Queen. I wished to 15 greet them very politely. They were very kind to me, but I had many problems when I tried to find a house or somewhere to sleep.

Three days after I had arrived in Blefuscu I went for a walk by the shore. In the sea, about half a mile away, 20 I saw a strange thing. I pulled off my shoes and socks and walked into the sea to take a look at it. It was a real European boat. But the bottom side was on top! Perhaps it had been lost from a large ship during a storm.

Bringing the boat to the shore

I returned to the beach. I asked the King to let me have twenty ships and three thousand seamen to help me. He agreed and they sailed around the coast to meet me.
5 I walked back to the shore. The sea had carried the strange boat nearer. I went into the water again. I swam behind the boat. Then with one hand I pushed it and with the other hand I swam along. Soon the water only reached my neck so I could stand up.

10 The seamen had made many ropes for me and I had twisted them together to make them stronger. They fastened the ropes to nine of their ships. Then they threw the ropes to me. I fastened the ends of the ropes to my boat.

15 The ships pulled the boat, and I pushed it. We moved it very near to the shore. I waited until the water was low. Then two thousand men with ropes and machines helped me to turn the boat over. I could not see much damage.

20 Later, and after I had worked very hard to mend the boat, I rowed into the harbour of Blefuscu. Thousands of people came to watch. It was the biggest boat they had ever seen.

A message from Lilliput

25 I told the King of Blefuscu that I was very lucky to find this boat. I begged him to allow me to mend it. Then I could use it to go back to my own country if I received his permission to leave Blefuscu.

I did not receive any messages from Lilliput at this
30 time. Someone told me that the Emperor of Lilliput thought that I would return there. He thought I did not know about his cruel plans for me. Later, he sent a

messenger to the King of Blefuscu.

'I must tell the Man-Mountain,' this messenger said, 'that if he will return to Lilliput, the Emperor will be very kind. He will only take away his eyes. My master wants you, the King of Blefuscu, to send back this Man-Mountain. But first, his hands and feet must be tied together.'

The King of Blefuscu thought about these words for a few days. He asked his officers to advise him. Then he sent this message to Lilliput.

'It is too difficult for us to return this man to you. If we tie his hands and feet we cannot move him. He has found a boat which is the right size for him. We will allow him to go to his own country. It costs both our countries too much to feed him and to look after him. This is the best plan.'

I get ready to leave

When I heard about these messages I decided to leave quickly. Five hundred workmen made two sails for my boat. They sewed thirteen pieces of their strongest cotton, one on top of the other. I twisted together twenty or thirty of their thickest ropes which made one good rope for me. On the seashore I found a large stone. I could use this as a very good anchor. The fat from three hundred sheep was rubbed on my boat. This was to stop any sea water from getting inside.

It took about a month to get everything ready. Then I went to say goodbye to the King and his family.

All of them came outside their beautiful home. I kissed the hand of the King, his Queen and the princes. His Majesty gave me fifty purses. In each purse there were two hundred gold coins. He handed me a picture of himself, which I put away carefully.

In the boat I carried the bodies of one hundred cows and three hundred sheep. I also put in some bread and wine as well as some cooked meat.

5 I wanted to show the animals of Blefuscu to the people of my own country, so I took some live animals with me. I also had to take dried grass and other special food to give them.

The King made me promise that I would not take away any of his people. He looked in all my pockets
10 before he gave me permission to leave.

A ship finds me

I sailed away at six o'clock in the morning on 24th September 1701. After my boat had sailed about twelve miles I noticed a small island. It was then about six
15 o'clock in the evening of the same day. I could not see any people so I put down my anchor. I ate some food and then I went to sleep.

When I woke up it was still dark. I ate some more food. Then I pulled up the anchor and I sailed to the
20 north again. I did not see anything all that day. On the third day I saw a ship's sail a long way away. I was afraid that no one would notice me. But the ship came nearer. Then I saw that it was sailing straight towards me. It came closer and closer. I was so happy. My heart
25 was full of hope that, at last, I should see my country and my dear family again.

Between five and six o'clock in the evening of 26th September I came along the side of the ship. I could see that it was a British ship. I put the cows and sheep in
30 my pocket. I picked up my food. I was ready to leave my little boat. I took as much as I could with me. Someone threw a rope ladder over the side, and I climbed up on to the ship.

I talk of my life in Lilliput

The name of the captain, the chief seaman, was John Biddell. He and his fifty men had been to Japan. They were returning to England through the South Seas. The ship's doctor was an old friend called Peter Williams. 5 He greeted me and he told Captain Biddell all about me. Captain Biddell was most kind to me. He asked many questions. Where had I come from? Where was I going?

I told him about everything that had happened to me. At first, when I told him I had been living in a 10 country where the people were no more than six inches tall, he thought that I was mad. He thought that the dangers in Lilliput and Blefuscu had made me ill.

Then I took the cows and sheep out of my pocket. He 15 was very surprised. He could not believe his eyes. I showed him the gold coins from Blefuscu and also the picture of the King. At last Captain Biddell believed me. I gave him two purses with two hundred gold coins in each of them. I promised to give him a cow and a 20 sheep when we arrived in England.

I had to look after these little animals. I had brought some food for them with me, but it did not last long. Then the Captain said I should try using the food the seamen ate. It was a kind of hard cake, called a biscuit. The captain gave me some of his best biscuits. I broke them into powder, mixed them with water, and gave this food to the animals. They quite liked it, which was good because there was nothing else for them to eat.

It was 13th April 1702 when we reached England. Almost all my animals arrived safely. I only lost one sheep which had been eaten by a rat. As soon as I could, I found a place where the grass was thick, but not too tall, and they began to eat at once. I was happy to see this. I thought that the long journey might have made them ill.

I go on another journey

I showed these small animals to many people in England. Everyone, rich and poor, wanted to see them. In this way I made a lot of money. When I left England for my next voyage, I sold them for six hundred pounds.

I stayed only two months with my wife and family. Then I felt that I had to see more foreign countries. Perhaps there were other places in the world where the people were as small as the Lilliputians. Perhaps there were even stranger things to see.

I bought a good house for my wife and I left one thousand and five hundred pounds with her. My uncle had given me some land north of London, and every year people paid me thirty pounds to use it. I also had a small shop from which I received even more money each year. So my wife and family had plenty to live on.

Johnny, my son, was doing well at school and my daughter, Betty, stayed at home with her mother. She liked to sew and to look after things in the house. Now, of course, she is married, and has children of her own. When I said goodbye to my dear wife and children we were all sad, and everyone cried. 5

I got work on a ship called the *Adventure* which was sailing from Liverpool to Surat, in India. I took some goods with me, and some money. I thought that I would be able to sell the goods at a high price in places that were far away from England, and make myself a little richer. But most of all I looked forward to seeing new lands and finding out about new people. 10

Questions and Activities

1 A Ship's Doctor

Put these sentences in the right order.

1 Gulliver went to study at Cambridge. ☐
2 He returned to London and married Mary Burton. ☐
3 Then he studied at Leyden in Holland for two years. ☐
4 He worked in London again, near a great harbour. ☐
5 He did not earn enough money for his family. ☐
6 He worked as a ship's doctor on the *Swallow*. ☐
7 After two years, he travelled again for six years. ☐
8 He got work as a ship's doctor on the *Antelope*. ☐
9 He went to London and worked for Dr Bates. ☐

2 A Prisoner

Fill in the gaps with the words from the box.

arrows	free	needles	spears
clothes	jacket	order	stakes

Gulliver tried hard to get (1) _____ . He pulled up

some of the (2) _____ . The little people ran away.

Then someone shouted an (3) _____ . About one

hundred (4) _____ were shot through the air

at Gulliver. Some of the little men tried to push

their (5) _____ into him. Gulliver did not feel

the arrows that went into his (6) _____ . The

spears were not sharp enough to go through his

(7) _____ . But the arrows that hit his face felt

like sharp (8) _____ .

3   The Journey to the City

*Put the letters of these words in the right order. The
first one has been done for you.*

The little people planned to take Gulliver to the

(1) **tipacal** city. They used the (2) **gentrosts** and biggest

capital

(3) **delehew** machine in the (4) **gidmonk**. When

Gulliver was (5) **pesale**, the little people brought the

machine close to his side. They used sticks with

(6) **lepsuly** and strong ropes to lift him off the

(7) **ondurg**. Then the machine was moved under him.

They put him down on the (8) **maltprof**, very

(9) **tyngle**. Gulliver did not wake up.

4   **The Emperor of Lilliput**

Find ten mistakes in this description of the Emperor.

The Emperor of Lilliput was shorter than any of his noblemen by about an inch. He was a bad rider. He did not fall when his dog got frightened. His face showed that he was weak and brave. He moved in a light and clumsy way. He was thirty-eight years old, which people in that country thought was quite young. He had been emperor for seven months. He had ruled his city happily and well.

5   **Inside Gulliver's Pockets**

Match the names of the things found in Gulliver's pockets with the right descriptions.

1 letters •

2 a comb •

3 a gun •

4 coins •

5 a watch •

• a A long piece of iron with a hole going through it.

• b A machine shaped like a flat ball that sounded like a heart beating.

• c Some stiff white sheets with strange black marks on them.

• d A machine made of twenty long sticks fixed to a longer, thicker stick.

• e Pieces of silver and red-brown metal, round and flat like plates.

6 **Free at Last**

Put the words in brackets in the right order.

1 The city of Milendo is [an] [square] [built] [exact] [in]

  The city of Milendo is built in an exact square

  _____.

2 There are many lanes, [to] [twelve] [wide] [inches]
  [eighteen]

  _____

  _____.

3 [have] [houses] [Some] [five] [as] [as] [floors] [many]

  _____

  _____.

4 [palace] [in] [is] [The] [the] [city] [centre] [the] [of]

  _____

  _____.

5 [shaped] [is] [It] [a] [square] [big] [like] [open]

  _____

  _____.

6 [rooms] [Emperor's] [The] [smallest] [in] [the]
  [building] [are]

  _____

  _____.

7 The War

Which of these sentences are true, and which are false?

                           T F

1 Gulliver used his spectacles to look towards Blefuscu.

2 He could see about fifty warships in a small harbour.

3 He made ropes and hooks, and then swam to Blefuscu.

4 He broke the anchor ropes at the front of the ships.

5 He pulled the enemy ships back to Lilliput.

6 He was given a title which means 'Little Nobleman'.

7 He was asked to bring all Lilliputian ships to Blefuscu.

8 He was so angry that he left the country.

9 He put out the fire in the room belonging to the Empress.

10 He was rewarded by the Empress for saving her life.

8 Laws and Customs

Circle the right words to say how children are treated in Lilliput.

In Lilliput, when the children are (1) **twelve/twenty** months old, they are taken from their

(2) **parents/friends**. They are looked after by special nurses and (3) **doctors/teachers**. The parents can only see their children twice a (4) **week/year**. They cannot even whisper (5) **kind/unkind** words to them.

9 The Man-Mountain is in Danger

Complete the reasons why the noblemen wanted to kill Gulliver.

1 He did not destroy •   • **a** Blefuscu.

2 He might fill the •   • **b** the palace
   palace with water   gardens.

3 He had spat on •   • **c** too much
                                         money.

4 He was planning •   • **d** all the ships
   to visit   of Blefuscu.

5 His food cost •   • **e** and drown
                                         everyone.

10 Gulliver Returns to England

Complete the crossword puzzle.

Gulliver found a (1) boat. The seamen helped him bring it to the (2). The King of Blefuscu let him (3) the boat so that he could (4) back to his own country. The King gave him fifty (5) with two hundred gold (6) in each purse. He also gave him a (7) of (8). For food, Gulliver took one hundred cows, three hundred (9), some bread, some wine and some cooked meat.

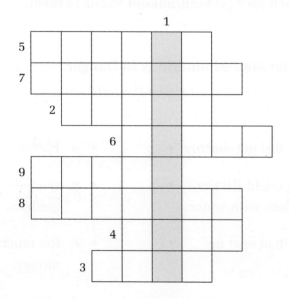

Book Report

Now write a book report to display in the library or your classroom. These questions will help you.

Title

Type What type of story is your book?

- Adventure
- Classic
- Crime
- Detective story
- Fairy tale
- Horror and suspense
- Mystery
- Play
- Romance
- Science fiction and fantasy
- Short story
- Others

Characters — Who are the main characters in the book?

Main characters — Describe the main characters.
What do they look like?
What are they like?

Story — What is the story about?
Remember not to give the ending away!

My comments — What did you think of the story?
Did you enjoy it?
Would you recommend this book to your classmates?

Visit the website and download the book report template
www.oupchina.com.hk/elt/oper

Starter

The Ant and the Grasshopper and Other Stories by Aesop
Retold by David Foulds

The Brave Little Tailor and Other Stories by the Brothers Grimm
Retold by Katherine Mattock

The Emperor's New Clothes and Other Stories by Hans Christian Andersen
Retold by Janice Tibbetts

Folk Tales from Around the World
Retold by Rosemary Border

Giants, Dragons and Other Magical Creatures
Retold by Philip Popescu

Heroes and Heroines
Retold by Philip Popescu

In the Land of the Gods
Retold by Magnus Norberg

Journey to the West
Retold by Rosemary Border

The Lion and the Mouse and Other Stories by Aesop
Retold by David Foulds

The Little Mermaid and Other Stories by Hans Christian Andersen
Retold by Janice Tibbetts

The Monkey King
Retold by Rosemary Border

Peter Pan
Retold by Katherine Mattock